Another Standard / Comedia

CULTURE AND DEMOCRACY

THE MANIFESTO

Comedia Publishing Group
9 Poland Street
London W1V 3DG
Tel: 01 439 2059

Comedia Publishing Group was set up to investigate and monitor the media in Britain and abroad. The aim of the project is to provide basic information, investigate problem areas, and to share the experiences of those working in the field, while encouraging debate about the future development of the media. The opinions expressed in the books in the Comedia series are those of the authors, and do not necessarily reflect the views of Comedia.

For a list of other Comedia titles see the back pages.

First published in 1986 by Comedia Publishing Group & The Shelton Trust.
© Comedia Publishing Group and The Shelton Trust, 1986.
Where we can collaborate democratically in the expression of these ideas, copyright will always be waived.

ISBN 1 85178 020 3 (paperback)

Typeset at Cultural Partnerships Limited, 90 De Beauvoir Road, London N1, using an Apple Macintosh and a Laserwriter.

Printed at Redesign, 9 London Lane, London E8.

Trade distribution by George Philip Services,
Arndale Road, Wick, Littlehampton, West Sussex BN17 7EN.

Distributed in Australia by Second Back Row Press,
50 Govett Street, Katoomba, New South Wales 2780

Distributed in Canada by DEC, 229 College Street, Toronto, Ontario, Canada M5T 1RA.

Remember. All those people who talk about revolution and class struggle
without refering *explicitly* to the positive power of refusal
and the politics of everyday life -
such people have a corpse in their mouth.

Wah! Heat

CONTENTS

This manifesto has been organised by a group of members of the Shelton Trust, as part of the Trust's contribution to a debate which has been gathering momentum for at least five years. Specifically, it has been written as a discussion paper for Another Standard 86: Culture & Democracy, a Conference taking place on July 12th and 13th 1986 in Sheffield. This conference is itself a staging post in a movement to establish cultural alliances which can set the agenda for political and social change.

The Shelton Trust began in 1979, as a national organisation of community artists, and has grown to embrace a wide range of cultural workers and activists. During that period it has moved from a concern with radicalising 'the arts' to a recognition that it is the operation of a dominant hierarchical culture that causes and sustains oppression in this society. That oppression underlies all areas of cultural work. Our desire to oppose and change this dominant culture is inseparable from the desire to change the political and economic systems which direct and perpetrate it.

Out of this recognition has come the development of a framework of ideas we call cultural democracy. This is not concerned directly with the day-to-day practices of cultural activists. Rather it addresses the aims of their work, and the work of the many thousands of others working to similar ends.

This manifesto is written from our experience, and locates that experience within a larger context of society. It is concerned, in some small part, with 'the arts'. However, it is not, in any sense, the basis for a

'campaign for the arts'. It is a specification for socialism based in a common analysis of politics, economics *and* culture.

Our aim is the creation of an egalitarian and plural society, by the extension of democratic practice to all social relationships.

Cultural democracy offers an analysis of the cultural, political and economic systems which dominate in Britain. More importantly, it offers a tool for action.

Effective action is impossible without understanding. Control of culture by a small group is not control of thought directly. Rather it is the control of the ability to use thought and understanding. Culture, at any one time, is the agenda of what is imagined to be possible. Culture is not simply the evidence of an unequal economic system. Culture is its foundation, its support, its means of justification and influence, and the context within which that system sustains itself.

Britain is highly centralised. Ownership remains concentrated in the hands of very small numbers of people Government works by creating and per- petrating an exclusive and inaccessible hierarchy. The same is true both of the powerful professions and the media. Together they transmit a culture which originates in the power of a few but through which all the population are instructed to live.

At any one time this powerful few can be crudely referred to as 'the ruling class'. This class can be identified with a group or groups of people - the landed aristocracy, wealthy business people, top politicians and media celebrities. While entrance is not necessarily hereditary, it always revolves around the acquisition and protection of wealth.

The power of these ruling classes is rooted in economic power, but it is not limited to this sphere.

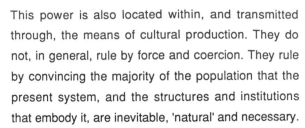

This power is also located within, and transmitted through, the means of cultural production. They do not, in general, rule by force and coercion. They rule by convincing the majority of the population that the present system, and the structures and institutions that embody it, are inevitable, 'natural' and necessary.

They do this through a process of oppression, in which the majority are convinced that what they want, what they think they need, is less important than what they are told will be made available to them. In this way people are encouraged to collude in their own oppression, and rewarded for doing so. This manifesto recognises that oppression, and its effects on the possibilities of an emerging socialism.

We believe that socialists must develop a coherent view of culture. We cannot afford merely to respond to dominant right-wing individualism by arguing for a bit more of this and a bit less of that. Instead we must produce a positive understanding and practice which arise from a different, a socialist, view of the role that culture plays under capitalism, and the role it plays as a vital part of a democratic socialism.

This manifesto is in two parts. The first part, *The State We're In*, provides a short analysis of some of the dominant forces which shape, and will shape, British society. We do not believe that these forces differ, in their underlying motivations and mechanisms, from the forces which shape and determine other 'first world' capitalist societies.

This section begins by looking at some of the defining characteristics of government, which are

related to interlocking networks of professional codes and practices. It then looks at the avenues of expression available to the majority of people, and the dynamics of cultural oppression with which people contend. It examines the dominant culture and value systems that underpin these systems of oppression, and relates these to the economic system that legitimises their continued existence.

The second section proposes another standard by which a socialism which linked political and cultural activism might move forward. It defines a concept of cultural democracy, linked to democratic values, and proposes a number of critcria for an effective opposition to the dominant hierarchical culture. Finally it lays out the basis for deciding on practical political aims.

It is in the nature of these aims that they must be decided democratically, by those groups and alliances which commit themselves to their achievement.

There are a number of key words which recur throughout the manifesto. We define here the way that we intend to use them.

We use the word *culture* to indicate social activity that creates, communicates or sustains social value. However, we refer here only to those activities which *predominantly* create and sustain social meaning. We include in this all forms of public communication.

We use the word *politics* to mean the administering and organising of all forms of activity between people. We do not just refer to the activities

11

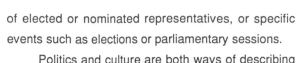

of elected or nominated representatives, or specific events such as elections or parliamentary sessions.

Politics and culture are both ways of describing social activity. They are not separate and containable activities that are voluntary or optional, and from which people can be excluded or can exclude themselves. They are not something that can be added to, or taken away from, social relationships. On the contrary, they are the defining characteristics of such relationships.

All people exist within, and are part of, numerous cultures, and all cultures are political. We are all concerned, individually and in common with others, to establish our own views and to express our understandings and our ways of life. The degree to which any of us are successful, and the ways in which we are successful, lies in how far our cultures are democratic.

We use the word to mean direct participation and shared power on an open and accountable basis. *Democracy*, then, is an analysis of culture and politics. It can, and should, operate in any area of society from the conduct of personal relationships to the control of the base of industrial production.

We believe that socialism is built through a process of deepening and extending democracy. Movement towards cultural democracy is its core.

SECTION ONE

The State we're in

Cultural life in Britain takes place within capitalism. This serves to limit the extent and curtail the forms that life can take. However, we believe the nature of capitalism has been completely misrepresented by *all* the major political parties. Often this has been a deliberate political strategy. Sometimes it has been the result of ignorance. Always it has resulted in possibilities for real change, possibilities for a genuinely democratic society, being stifled or curtailed.

We intend to examine briefly some key features of the state of Britain, before outlining a basis for moving towards these democratic possibilities. We begin with the nature of government.

We are governed at many levels. The United Nations, the EEC, The House of Commons, the House of Lords, local councils, education authorities, health authorities, police authorities, urban development corporations, regional authorities, the monopolistic utilities (gas, water, electricity), the Bank of England, the Church of England, the three arms of the military, arts associations, broadcasting authorities, transport authorities, the judiciary, and many bodies from the Office of Fair Trading to the DHSS and the Industrial Tribunals all exercise power over our lives, whether we like it or not.

Although our government is alleged to be democratic, the majority of those bodies that have power to control, direct and influence us are not elected. The membership of most of them is appointed privately, often through mechanisms which

GOVERNMENT

are themselves hidden from us. Professional groups such as barristers are self-selecting, and powerful voluntary groups, from magistrates to Arts Council members, are selected without public accountability, often as 'experts' from informal lists of 'the great and the good'.

Most formal bodies operate through invitation, in this way, just as most governing institutions are headed by appointed boards. The same is true, in practice, for the boards of companies. Size of shareholding (that is, the effective ability of the rich to purchase an invitation) is the deciding factor in election by shareholders.

These hidden structures exist equally in all walks of 'public life', and ensure the 'suitability' of appointees. The public criteria emerge as 'experience', 'fairmindedness', 'education' and so on. The hidden criteria ensure that their effect is to support institutions against the incursion of wider experience and public scrutiny. Moreover, even where the membership of public bodies *is* elected there is no mechanism to require members to consult, involve or remain accountable to their constituencies.

Yet this lack of real public control and access remains largely unnoticed. The exercise of power is regularly described in ways which make it appear dull, incomprehensible and remote. This distance, this lack of clarity, is portrayed as 'normal', as is the lack of scrutiny which inevitably accompanies it. Although it is sometimes pretended otherwise, government is separate from the interests and concerns of the population; except briefly at election times, when a

DEMOCRACY

CREATES

VALUE

CAPITALISM

SELLS IT

minority of the population choose between the candidates made available to them.

What accountability there is within government operates upwards and inwards, towards a smaller group of more powerful people, rather than outwards towards the rest of the population. The absence of any direct and accountable connection with 'the public', has allowed the growth of systems of *informal control* within the institutions of government. When we vote for a programme of legislation, we later find that its effects are very different from those we intended. This occurs because of the influences of those systems of lobbying and back-door negotiation which constitute the real mechanisms of control, and because there is no system for making clear what a proposal will mean in practice.

Currently voting serves simply to set in train a long, and often secret series of bureaucratic mechanisms. What happens then remains hidden until the results finally become public.

'Justice' is no more democratic than the political system which currently, and fraudulently, represents itself as such. Barristers are called to the bar by other barristers, judges are chosen by other judges, lawyers are policed by their own organisation, the Law Society; and at the top of the pile sits the unelected Lord Chancellor.

Indeed the development of 'justice', in response to powerful interests, is frequently oppressive, first in specific terms and then much more generally. Laws are enacted and instituted as an answer to the immediate needs of those who

16

designate themselves as 'responsible' for the nation, but they also serve to add to the structure of control and oppression.

The licensing laws, for example, were first introduced to cut down on key workers' alleged drinking during the First World War, but have grown into a major instrument of social regimentation. The Prevention of Terrorism Act allowed the pioneering of policing techniques in Northern Ireland which were later introduced into England.

Law-making in British society habitually preoccupies itself with preventing people combining freely, except in licensed or officially permitted groups. It has also been obsessed with controlling freedom of movement. This has been relaxed only in direct proportion to the increasing ability of governments and police forces to locate and identify individuals. The ability of individuals to move freely has been accompanied by a whole array of devices to keep track of people - from the Inland Revenue's records to National Insurance numbers and passports. Where these have been administered separately, information technology increasingly makes possible their coordination for policy purposes.

This system is not neutral. Everybody is not free to participate on an equal basis. It has been built by the most powerful groups within society reflecting their interests. Government usurps the power of the electorate and acts not on its behalf but in its stead. Public servants have become slavemasters. What is promoted as representative democracy ends up as no democracy at all, but a liberal oligarchy.

PROFESSIONAL POWER

The institutions and structures of government, although immensely powerful, are themselves only a small part of the forces which act on us, with or without our permission. Some of the others wield direct economic power, but mostly their power is more subtle. In the main they are concerned with the mechanisms through which our lives are regulated, controlled and directed.

Professionalism is one of these forces. Much of the decision-making in this society is in the hands of people who are judged more competent than the majority of the population, because of the status their profession is accorded. Usually this status is enforced by law, either directly or by the legally granted power to issue licences and certificates. A passport application, for example, must be countersigned by a member of an officially recognised profession, with the result that the wealthy and 'educated' get their friends to sign while 'ordinary' people have to pay a doctor or solicitor a fee to have it done.

Many of the powers professionals exercise are unaccountable and self-regulatory. Moreover access to the relevant skills is deliberately restricted, and often directly forbidden for anyone other than a licensed professional. The power of the professions depends on their ability to maintain a monopoly over a range of often quite simple tasks, and to act to prevent others undertaking them.

In professions ranging from the health service, the army, the police force, to the broadcasting networks and the newspaper industry, decisions

which occur at the top of a professional hierarchy are used subsequently to validate the professional operation of the hierarchy. We are told, for example, that television news reports are generally fair and unbiased because the institutional structure ensures that this is so. The BBC was established by government, as was the IBA. They are said by broadcasters to be independent of the system by which they were set up. This fiction supports the belief that professionalism is objective by self-definition.

Professionalism operates without reference to the individual feelings of those professionals within it. Professionals may not personally support or believe in the values of the ruling culture, but their work nonetheless transmits these values, because they Implement Ideas which have already been enacted elsewhere. A gynaecologist may be personally sympathetic to the needs of women in childbirth, and may even be able to change local medical practice considerably. She is not, however, in any real sense, accountable to those women, except where she may be proven in law to have made mistakes. Moreover the women with whom she works have no power to insist that she work as she does. They are simply lucky that she chooses to do so.

Although dedicated and 'radical' professionals may be able to affect local practices, they are unable to unable to change or redirect the overall direction and resourcing of the service to which they belong. The needs of consumers are subordinated to the practices and beliefs of the professionals, which are themselves contained by government of that hierarchy.

Within this system, there exists a powerful assumption that need is not definable by those who have the need. Need is only definable by those who have received a long and specialised education, and are usually members of a professional association that regulates the definition of other's needs. In fact, these 'needs' usually have much more to do with the history and internal logic of professional practices, and the capitalism within which they operate, than with any social expression of needs. Poverty is defined by economists, academics and journalists; by anybody but those who experience poverty. 'Standards' have over-ridden people's own definitions of need.

To be 'ordinary' within this system is to be disenfranchised in every area except the most general. Only at elections do 'ordinary' people have power, and in elections there are no opportunities to comment on specific issues, no opportunities to make anything but the most general of comments.

This system has been constructed during, and as a part of, the growth of capitalism.It is neither an accident nor a conspiracy, in the usual sense of that word. It has been assembled slowly over time, through the constant modification of behaviour, actions and methods of licensing, some of which were deliberately planned and some of which were unplanned or had unforeseen consequences. Indeed it is still being assembled, for it is not the sort of system that is ever 'finished'. This is its strength, and the reason that it is so powerful and so inimical to

20

democracy.

Decision making is hidden, and social needs are redefined as administrative problems. The effect of this is to deny the majority of citizens the ability to participate in defining their own needs.

EXPRESSION & OPPRESSION

The mechanisms of governmental and professional power are bolstered by a number of assumptions about the ways in which ideas are formed and made public, and about the ways in which decisions are reached and ratified. These are used to justify the present system, often by arguing that this system is somehow inevitable, or that the mechanisms that underpin it are 'common-sense'. These assumptions promote a particular view.

Forms of expression that people use vary from group to group, community to community, class to class, but they share common features. Where expression occurs between equals the terms on which it occurs are explicit, and personally understandable. The people involved make sense of what they learn, because they, literally, know what is going on.

In relationships where the terms are hidden, however, what occurs is not expressive, but oppressive. Rather than gaining knowledge through a process in which the terms are understood, people operate in the dark, picking up incomplete information the sources of which remain hidden. Many different groups of people are oppressed in this way. A majority of the population faces some form of oppression in the extent to which they have opportunities to address their own needs directly.

When we read something in a newspaper, for example, we are taught to believe that it is the same kind of expression we experience in our daily lives. It isn't. It is not a personal expression, the bias of which

we can recognise, understand and allow for; and from which we can form opinions or gain knowledge. Rather it is the professional work of a journalist and it already contains opinions and bias embedded within it. This professionalised information is presented as though it were raw data, but it has, in fact, been selected by a particular class of professionals to provide a particular range of views.

When the Peacock Committee was considering the future of the BBC, the *Times* ran many editorials and articles stressing the need to break up this unwieldy and unnecessary monopoly. This information comletely changes character if one realises that Rupert Murdoch has a large financial interest in television companies which would directly and greatly benefit from the dismantling of the BBC.

This kind of information is external to the reader. The choices it offers are spurious, for people can only use it to form a point of view which has effectively been predetermined by the pre-packaged range that is offered. Moreover, the criteria used in the construction of this range of views are concerned, directly or indirectly, with profitability.

The concern of the professionals involved is, at one level or another, with a form of presentation which keep people buying (and watching or listening or reading). Information, therefore , comes in the form of 'stories' about personalities, and not in the form of developed arguments about issues. Active choice is rendered unlikely, and participation in the creation of public opinion is removed from the agenda.

No 'ordinary' person, libelled by a national

newspaper, can afford to seek redress in the courts. There is no legal aid available for this purpose. From this perspective, the owners of newspapers, whether individuals or corporations, can be seen to own the means to create social meaning. It is unimportant whether or not the *Sun* or the *Mirror* support a particular issue. What matters is their power to define the range of views that will be deemed 'legitimate' around any issue, and their related ability to undermine popular belief in any alternative view.

This power is maintained by the power of wealth. Directly, it is maintained by the ability of large companies to undercut smaller competitors and thus force them out of business. If you have no purchasing power, you have no voice and thus no purchasing power. Indirectly, it is maintained by the kind of expensive lobbying which results in licensing regulations, and legal frameworks which work to their advantage,

Such concentrations of power are fundamentally undemocratic because they create and sustain a specific view of society in a way which cannot easily be challenged. The means to propogate opinions publicly through the media is literally owned by a small number of rich men, whose culture has mobilised and used the structure of the law to support, maintain and develop a monopoly.

24

DOMINANT CULTURE

The mechanisms of oppression interlock to form a dominant culture. We are displaced from the centre of our lives. We learn through sophisticated and often apparently congenial means that Britain is 'our culture, our society' and that we both participate in it and benefit from it, even though in fact a majority of people may be thinking and feeling otherwise. From the values it promotes and the symbols it uses in this promotion we learn to define our expectations and interpret our own lives. Personal experience becomes inferior, something not worth communicating or something that won't be heeded.

We receive rather than express, and take part in our own oppression by acting uncritically on received desires, values and stereotypes. These serve to divert attention from the complexities of interaction to the simplicities of an externally directed culture. The perennial enthusiasm which is fostered for 'our heritage' is an example of one such stereotype. It points attention backwards and undermines all activity except that which conforms to what is classified officially as 'culture'. It does this by affirming the official version of history and then romanticising it. This determines the agenda of references for the future.

It is ironic, then, that the guardians and curators of this 'official' culture regularly remark on the propensity of totalitarian states to falsify history, as though the history they teach is absolute, objective and universal, and all their records are a 'true' representation of the past. In so doing they hide the

DEMOCRACY

PROPOSES

CITIZENSHIP ·

CAPITALISM

DEMANDS

CONSUMERS

fact that British culture also performs this function, but in a way which disguises the fact. The heritage of the ruling class is the oppression, even the slavery of other classes and other nations.

The history which comprises 'our heritage' is not in any way objective. It has been written by those groups occupying the positions of power which enable them to shape public knowledge. These are also the groups with most to protect. The effect of a popular acquiescence in the idea of 'our heritage' - what 'we' did yesterday, rather than what is to be done now - is the same as the effect that the monopolist media generate. It defines what is valuable, while identifying the people that own it in as anodyne a way as possible.

Any opposition to the prevailing standards, therefore, seems to have less validity than the dominant culture it opposes. It seems less real, less solid, less known, less reliable, less 'British'. Political action has a stigma attached to it. To organise against the status quo implies going against a 'natural order' of things, and therefore implies defying 'common sense'. Any group which seeks to establish its own identity, based around its own definition of its needs is disadvantaged from the outset.

These received ideas affect us all. We are affected by how far we feel these ideas to be accessible or resistable and by how far we believe our feelings to be shared. The dominant culture promotes particular images and demotes others. It manipulates feeling by invoking ideas of worth which the vast majority of citizens have had no part in creating.

26

The ability to name and to define is a key tool for those who control the dominant culture. Naming confers power. This power flows from ownership of the means to propogate and promote those definitions. It permits the creation of image, identity, social value and status. It is a process of judgement, which authorises and legitimises some things while demoting and dismissing others. This power is applied across a whole range of social activities and arrangements.

Ownership, access and distribution permit the making of categorical and apparently absolute statements on the basis of their being 'informed' and 'independent' judgements. These exemplify 'excellence'; what is most desirable, most suitable and least challenging to the interests of the dominant cultures.

The culture of those who are most powerful is manifest. We need to remind ourselves, for example, that the Hammer Beam roof in Westminster Hall was made by numerous skilled working people and not by the monarchs and politicians whose names are associated with the building. It is remembered for its association with personal power rather than collaborative skill. The workers who made it had no say in what they were building or the purpose to which it would be put and the workers' names, the records of their lives are lost, if indeed they were ever recorded.

Official history comprises the legacy of the power of ruling classes to name, realised in the actions and artefacts named. Both have values deriving from their creators, but the values attached

STYLE

WITHOUT

FASHION

IS THE

IMAGINATION

OF

DEMOCRACY

to those who initiated, commissioned or bought them are imposed on them.

'Art', like 'heritage', is an ideological construction. Access to a position of power within society confers the ability to transmit value through personal taste. Ideas can be owned, and the promotion of one particular group of creative skills as 'art', and the simultaneous dismissal of all other such skills as mere 'crafts', is one way in which this ownership is enforced.

The whole edifice of production in this society is founded upon this separation of activity from purpose. To be placed outside the ambit of approved definitions is almost invariably to be deprived of any form of public distribution. Expression in a vacuum is no expression at all. It is a bewildering oppression, of a sort which has been applied systematically during the development of capitalism to 'art', to women, to minorities of all kinds and to other societies.

These mechanisms are designed to promote one particular set of values at the expense of all others. They aim to make impossible the existence and development of other sets of values, particularly those arising from other cultures. They aim, moreover, to sustain those who promote them.

28

DOMINANT VALUES

Dominant culture is underpinned by a set of values, some of which are codified in law and some of which are promoted informally. It is justified by the notion that these values, and the laws and regulations made in their name, are universal, timeless and absolute. In reality, however, laws are made and administered by the most powerful groups in society, and necessarily reflect and promote their interests. By this means those whose lives form and support the ruling culture impose *their* needs, *their* behaviour and *their* values on the rest of the population, while maintaining that these values are an objectivo measurement of civilised behaviour.

Particular ways of behaving are elevated into 'standards of behaviour', in a way which denigrates and disenfranchises the habits and ideas of other groups. In this way a uniform pattern of social expectations emerges, and we subscribe to or are forced to aspire to one set of values. Expectations are divorced from needs.

This process of separation is a central facet of the dominant culture, and one of the starting points for its system of values. People are separated from each other by professional intermediaries. Generalised information is superimposed on personal knowledge. Feeling is separated from action.

In this way individuals are encouraged to believe that they alone are responsible for their personal advancement. With the exception of those actions which are defined as criminal, it is, however, not viewed as their responsibility if this turns out to be at the expense of other people. Thus a system is created which maintains control by opening up distances between people, and then justifies itself by claiming that this distance is 'natural'.

The highly paid are depicted as 'top people', which inevitably implies the existence of 'bottom people'. Capitalism constructs an apparently 'natural' order; a pyramidal structure which is a social version of the survival of the fittest, in which a few hawks rule over many sparrows. This is the doctrine of individualism; a doctrine which is used to justify those ideas, values and beliefs which most suit the ruling groups in this society by dressing them up in an apparent objectivity.

The structure of language itself is subject to this, and is used to support apparent objectivity. Whenever the words are not there an idea or feeling will remain unstated. Language can be a door to understanding but it can also be a barrier preventing our access. It is a feature of an oppressive culture that language will consistently promote the interests of the most powerful. Language is never neutral. People who are oppressed, for example, are redefined as 'disadvantaged', in a way which immobilises them by reducing a political issue to a problem of administration.

The structure of society, the language that we are taught, combine to disenfranchise the majority of the population by promoting values - tools of understanding - that apparently mean one thing, but operate to another, unstated end.

Cultures may change considerably without

30

changing the central fact that there is a culture which dominates and imposes an oppressive standard, and that this ruling culture determines the opportunities and avenues of cultural expression for the majority of citizens. This is completely incompatible with democracy.

Dominant culture, and the system of dominant values which supports it, have been generated and sustained through economic power, connected to the changed, and changing, nature of the capitalism within which cultural life takes place.

Capitalism began as an economic system which industrialised the production and distribution of traditional goods from clothes, household and workplace implements to food. At this stage it was a way of producing, more profitably, what people already wanted, whether shirts, knives or cheese.

This process involved individual entrepreneurs developing, or paying to have developed, industrialised equivalents of traditional goods. Thus the soap that was produced industrially in the latter half of the nineteenth century was not the same as soap produced traditionally; but it was an analogous product capable of serving the same function as traditional soap.

The logic of capitalism, though, contains no idea of sufficiency. It is a system in which growth occurs for profit, and the generation of wealth becomes a value in its own right. There is no such thing as sufficient profit, and therefore no point at which a business, or an entrepeneur will have grown rich enough. Unlike physical hunger, a hunger for money and the power it brings, is never satiated.

For this reason capitalism did not cease growing when it had reached the point where it was capable of meeting the basic needs of food, shelter and clothing. It continued to generate products and

DOMINANT ECONOMICS

services, and began the simultaneous project of creating markets for them. It also began to encroach on more and more areas of social life, as it expanded from the production of simple, tangible goods to the capitalised delivery of services such as 'education' or 'health'.

As it did this, it necessarily moved from being a method of organising economic production to a method of ordering consciousness necessary for ever increasing production. The production of goods and services is ceasing to be its primary task. Instead this has become the production of markets whose stimulated 'needs' it canthen moot.

This is being achieved by a number of means. Firstly companies have tended to amalgamate or absorb each other, with the result that in most major areas of production there is an effective monopoly held by a small cartel. This monopoly has been able to define popular expectations by determining the choices that we will be allowed, and marketing what is essentially the same material in a variety of shapes and with a variety of calculatedly different images.

This monopolistic power has also enabled the promotion of a consensus view of, say, the necessity of using washing powder or shaving cream, or the normality and desirability of smoking cigarettes. From this perspective every advertisement for a family car is a piece of propaganda about the desirability of driving rather than taking the bus or train. Over and above the effect of a specific advertisement in selling us one or another car, we are sold the idea that we need a car, whatever brand we choose. It tells us that the

33

CULTURAL

DEMOCRACY

IS

A WAY

OF PUTTING

THE JIGSAW

TOGETHER

correct choice is between brands of cars rather than between buying a car or a bus pass.

Secondly capitalism has sought to break down needs into smaller and smaller units, in order that we can be taught to use a greater number of products and services to achieve the same effect. Thus the need to be healthy has been turned into a desire - a market - for dietary supplements, vitamin pills and body lotions. Even the desire to be thin, itself the subject of and at least partly the result of widespread promotion, is turned into a market for *additional* consumer goods, including low calorie foods and appetite suppressants.

Thirdly the provision of professional and other services have been capitalised, with the result that the number of professional intermediaries with the ability to exert profound effects on our lives has increased dramatically, and the market for their services is the subject of deliberate stimulation.

The mechanisms of stimulation arise as a part of the dominant culture and the values it promotes, and themselves serve to sustain and develop it. This culture is the medium through which the business of creating markets is managed and at the same time hidden from view. It also enables and underwrites the shaping and determining of popular expectations into the forms necessary for this business to happen.

Culture then is not something which happens on the fringes of capitalist economics. Its manipulation is the key to capitalism's continued growth, and hence its continued existence. Culture, therefore, cannot be an issue of peripheral concern to political activists,

34

whether socialist or not. It is a vital area for campaign and struggle. Capitalism is not bounded simply by politics and economics. Opposition which does not recognise this cannot be effective.

Opposition must also recognise capitalism's own transformation of itself. Rather than reacting to those structures capitalism has operated, it must anticipate and address control as it is now being exercised and developed.

Capitalism is dynamic. The masive potential of information technology is currently fuelling a transformation of control in the world's economies. Ownership of control is becoming more important than formal ownership of the means of production. Production is everywhere being diversified while control is being centralised, which weakens the industrial power of workers and the political control of nation states.

This applies to manufacturing, and it also applies to the creation of markets for multinational corporations. Tobacco companies are adapting to the increasing impact of legislation in OECD countries by transferring sales to new markets.

It also applies to the movement of wealth to capitalise and instate new forms of control. Computer and satellite technology can now move money beyond the ability of governmental exchange controls to restrict movement. This transnational operation cannot be controlled democratically, nor opposed by any conventional approaches to law, political organisation or government.

Industrial or economic activism, then, will be

DEMOCRACY WITHOUT SOCIALISM IS FORM WITHOUT CONTENT

futile without a parallel cultural activism, just as cultural activism which is not rooted in political and economic activism will be self-serving and trivial. Without cultural democracy, industrial or political democracy are merely abstract notions incapable of being put into practice. Together they are capable of bringing democracy into existence.

Another

Standard

Choice is never universal, but is always bounded by constraints some of which are practical and some ideological. All feelings and all opinions are particular, and arise from and relate directly to particular communities, classes and cultures. All culture is political and it works to the advantage of those who have the most opportunity to make choice because they exercise the most power.

The current mode of social organisation is unable to cope with any groups whose interests are different from its own, except in ways which are oppressive. It is unable to cope democratically, for example, with the demands made upon it by multiculturalism.

It updates imperialism in order to designate groups as minorities in need of help, or as aliens in need of civilising. It denies them any rights of participation in planning or administratiing their needs. Instead it arranges to act on their behalf and in their stead. White arts officers, for example, set up, and then subsequently staff, 'ethnic arts' committees rather than restructuring the institutions within which they work, so that they can become genuinely plural.

Moreover it exports this denial to the rest of the world. Multinational food companies, for example, create and then monopolise markets for food products that are entirely unrelated to expressed needs. Technical expertise that could be used to assist indigenous agriculture and make possible the local control of nutrition is used by the OECD nations to distort national economies in the Third World in

order to supply markets for animal feed crops. Productive capacity is diverted to support Western meat consumption, and the resulting gap is conveniently filled by imported baby foods, manufactured by the multinationals.

This process, like most of the social processes which surround us, happens in our name, although we are given no opportunity to shape, direct, control or prevent it. It serves as one of a multitude of examples, all of which indicate the profound need for a democratic system capable of permitting direct expressions of need, not by a private network of ruling groups, but by the majority of citizens.

It highlights the importance of building a political system which is genuinely and directly democratic, and which enables the majority of citizens to participate in the creation and maintenance of social rights. Within a democracy there can be no assumption that rights exist, for in a democracy there are no rights except for those which are openly and democratically made. Such a system depends on creation rather than assumption, on communication and expression rather than restriction and oppression.

A measure of the extent to which a society is democratic can be found in how far people feel that they are able to express their needs through participation in its administration; whether in choosing what they are able to buy when they go shopping or in planning public transport routes or even in going to war. In a genuine democracy people make their culture rather than have it made for to them - locally, nationally and internationally.

This is what we mean by cultural democracy. It is a continuous political system, which depends on exchange and collaboration. It depends on listening as well as telling. It is necessarily accessible to contributions from many sources, and it makes possible democratic movement through the building of social alliances. It is a process which begins from the proposition that democracy is impossible unless all the administrative systems within a society are themselves democratic, understandable and available for use by the majority of the population.

The ideas that constitute cultural democracy both enable and depend upon direct participation, and take as their aim the building and sustenance of a society in which people are free to come together to produce, distribute and receive the cultures they choose.

A culture that is genuinely democratic presupposes only flux and change. Political aims cannot be identified separately from the means to implement them. People make demands which lead to political objectives. When implemented these demands do not cease. They are contingent on the service received, and they condition the operation of this service.

Services must therefore be created and administrated in recognition of the democratic process, with the means of real democratic change built in. The point where a service is instituted is the point of closest contact with those whose demands

40

led to its creation. That sense of contact should be integral, from the moment of foundation to the regular working of the service. If it is not, then the service will not promote the values that supported its creation. It will atrophy in the minds of its users as they lose their sense of involvement, and as they continue to move forward while the service apparently stands still.

A society committed to cultural democracy, and to the industrial democracy and political democracy that must accompany it, will necessarily operate with different and open values and standards.

Dominant culture is energetically promoting individualism. The 'new individualism', it is alleged, will take society forward into a new era of 'popular capitalism'. What it will actually do, is to modernise and strengthen an existing framework of unequal social relationships, while leaving their basic principles untouched.

There is a crucial difference between the kind of individualism which is being promoted and *individuality*. The former is the product of, and itself supports, a system of oppressive values. It is an invitation to plan personal welfare, and access to the limited material gains which are desirable for personal welfare, to the exclusion of wider social concerns.

This individualism is irresponsible because it pretends that the individual can somehow be absolved of social responsibility. This kind of individualism abandons of any possibility of making common rights, in favour of a brutal scramble for whatever rights have been conceded by those groups that currently possess the power to define.

This irresponsibility supports the claims of the most powerful minorities to impose their desires on society, and have them legitimised as 'natural' needs, just as it effectively denies the possibility of reciprocal social relationships. It is in direct opposition to that form of responsibility which arises from a mutual recognition of needs and the consequent making of rights through the process of exchange.

We believe that values árise and are sustained and developed as part of a *social* process. They

occur within the relationships that exist and develop between people, and form a vital part of those relationships. Values are developed and legitimised through a process of negotiation.

We must seek to develop systems of values which are pluralistic. Values arise within communities, within groups of people, and they draw their strength and vitality from the life of these communities. We must find ways of enabling the values of different groups to coexist, without one oppressing the other.

A particular set of creative acts, 'the arts', identifies a small range of activity which has been chosen from an infinitely larger range. This choice represents the values of one particular class. It is the operation of an oppressive culture. We believe that *whatever* creative acts people participate in are important to those people, and are capable of producing the pleasures and insights usually attributed to 'the arts'.

'The arts' are a mechanism for awarding privileges to creative acts sanctioned by some powerful groups at the expense of all others. Bodies like the Arts Council of Great Britain are unelected ways of perpetrating this and should be abolished. They are by nature incapable of reform. From the perspective of cultural democracy, we believe it is important is ensuring that a plurality of cultural production is possible, that the resources for such activities are available in ways people can use, and that there exist distribution channels able and willing to distribute the wide variety of work that occurs.

The intellectual and administrative apparatus of 'arts' funding agencies are virtually unable to cope properly with any 'art' which does not have its ancestry in the Renaissance or the subsequent history of cosmopolitan European fine art. African performing arts, for example, are forced to redefine themselves as either music, poetry or dance, in order to fit into a dominant Eurocentric conception and thus meet the criteria of funding agencies.

When *all* people's creativity is taken seriously,

A CHANGED LANDSCAPE

the idea of 'cultural industries' is more useful than the idea of 'the arts', in which unaccountable funding bodies give out their 'prince's favours' to the lucky recipients of their 'expert' choice. A cultural industries strategy recognises that different groups of people express themselves in different ways, using differing forms. Further it is not the particular form used, but the seriousness of intent and the place that activity, and the products that result from it, occupy within the lives of communities. Funding, where necessary, should recognise intention, not the medium through which that intention is expressed.

Criteria for funding cultural activities which begin with a series of moral judgements about the place of certain activities within the 'High Arts' are not, and never can be, democratic. Whatever their apparent intention, they will always be oppressive.

From the starting point of cultural democracy questions of access to public buildings for people with disabilities cease to be issues of 'concern', which can be undertaken 'as soon as possible', and become what they truly are: basic questions of democratic rights. Such questions necessarily *precede* all considerations of constructing democratic leisure policies. They cannot merely be a part of such policies.

Without access to public buildings, large numbers of citizens have their freedom curtailed, are disenfranchised, and left unable to participate. The lack of availability of public transport and essential support services such as childcare curtail the freedom of further large groups of citizens in a way which is

FASHION WITHOUT STYLE IS THE POWER OF CAPITALISM

incompatible with democracy.

Britain's national newspapers are the personal property of eight wealthy men. 80% of periodicals are distributed through just three wholesalers, who effectively have between them the power to determine what magazines reach the public.

Democracy requires that monopolies be dismantled. It requires that the costs of such forms of production be lowered, and distribution systems built which allow people to influence what is distributed. It further requires that people have access to the producers while having the space to simply ignore them.

Socialism stands for the redistribution of wealth. To be democratic, it has to redistribute power. Centralisation results in a separation between a facility, a service, and those who produce and use it. Cultural democracy therefore proposes decentralisation, as a means of breaking down power, and preventing its accumulation in unassailable monopolies.

Decentralisation of cultural resources can be achieved without parochialism, establishing locally controlled production and distribution networks which allow people to exert active influence. Instead of centralised power which percolates downwards, cultural democracy rests upon a plurality of local powers which can choose to federate on a basis of reciprocal need, for example; to build roads, to provide networks of health care or to manufacture goods requiring a large scale of operation.

46

Any effective opposition must not merely propose another external 'political' system, but must work towards fundamentally different ways of feeling and living. We cannot use the language and practices of a 'capitalist, hierarchical, monarchical, sexist, racist, militarist' culture to propose, and organise for, its replacement. We cannot successfully comm-unicate the need to create democratic ways of living by using the values of a society which we recognise to be divisive, exploitative and oppressive.

We habitually refer to as the 'Labour Movement', yet it is in reality no such thing. It is a series of partially democratic structures which can, for instance, transmit sexist values every bit as well as the Conservative Party. When actually in government, the Labour Party did not create structures which promoted socialist values, and did not add to, or build on, progressive ideas such as the Co-operative movement embodied, but instead enacted reforms in much the same way as a nineteenth century Liberal government.

Nationalisation has been, in practice, merely economic reform of disorganised industries, in ways which put them under nominal state rather than 'private' ownership. The health service, for example, never came under direct democratic control and has, in consequence, been attacked successfully by subsequent governments, including the last Labour government and the present Thatcher governments. The electorate neither owns nor controls the health service. It has merely been told that it does, in

DEMOCRACY

IS

MANY STATES

OF MIND

NOT

THE MIND

OF THE STATE

contradiction of a legal and political system that recognises only power and not need.

The institutions that control the state are not the electorate, nor can they legitimately stand in for, or understudy, the electorate. The electorate, however, has no direct control over the mechanisms of the state. Voting is at best an occasional system of influence within which self-regulating political parties promote policy directions about which most of the population have no coherent knowledge. Moreover they are not provided with anything from which they could form such knowledge.

Any analysis of what we mean by 'left wing' must therefore begin with a fundamental reappraisal of our starting point. It must start with an understanding of how our present society operates; how the many structures and organisations, and the complex relationships between them, exist and have effect.

This requires examination, but this examination cannot claim to be final. It cannot be prescriptive, but must be prefigurative. It is a pulling together of many threads to create visible understanding that popular movements are political change.

A different 'left' politics needs to be created, where unitary political parties do not appropriate the struggle and experience of others in order to justify being representative. The forms of such a politics will develop through alliances, through direct combinations of different groups, not led but leading jointly.

48

The alliances we envisage will be conditional. That is to say, the groups involved will come together

around specific issues, without compromising their overall aims. They will not, then be a united front, which seeks to bury or hide differences, but will operate on the basis of constructive disagreement. These alliances will also be contingent. That is to say, they will depend upon the groups involved continuing to place the alliances on their lists of priorities. They will not be open-ended but rather will be explicitly renewed or cancelled at regular intervals.

Within these alliances any one static social analysis - class analysis, for example - will be recognised as oppressive wherever and whenever it seeks to be monopolistic. Women, gays and lesbians, Blacks and Asians, people with disabilities, and similar groups do not face harrassment or disadvantage because of class, but because of being female, gay, Black, Asian or disabled. However, this is not to say that people are not harrassed because they are working class.

To say that this oppression does not exist, or is somehow less or less important, if people are not working class, or to say that , if people are oppressed they must be working class, is itself oppressive. It limits and constrains identity, it cancels opportunities. for self-determination and it undermines the plurality of experience.

We must recognise that capitalism has developed beyond being a form of economic production, and is now predominantly a method of creating and sustaining the conditions necessary for that economic production to flourish and grow. Any movement that aims to be effective in proposing an

SOCIAL MARKETS ARE THE CULTURES OF POLITICAL MOVEMENTS

idea of society other than that promoted by capitalism must recognise that capitalism cannot be overthrown by activity which takes place solely in the sphere of economics or politics, because the organisation of the social system extends beyond these.

Actions in these spheres, undertaken in the belief that they are, on their own, 'revolutionary', will be doomed to failure. They will at best reform some of the surface aspects of the system, while leaving its core untouched. They can provide no radically effective opposition.

50

A FUTURE

Our politics should proceed from the recognition that oppression is not static but occurs *within* relationships. Indeed it could be said that oppression *is* the relationship between people in an oppressive society. Political goals are specific kinds of constantly occurring change, rather than static ends which in practice promote their own invisible agenda. We need a programme to promote a move from separation to communication, from *disconnected* passivity to *engaged* activity.

We must work to invert the oppressive logic of the current licensing and regulatory mechanisms. We must replace them with democratic processes capable of serving people's needs.

We must campaign for social structures which allow and encourage the right of access to the creation and distribution of ideas, feelings and beliefs. People must have a right to make themsleves heard, and to make their views and opinions public in ways which satisfy their perceived and expressed needs.

We must work for the decentralisation of cultural production and distribution. We must move from a system in which ideas and products are transmitted from centralising sources. We must argue for systems to support ideas and products which are produced and distributed from many local and regional sources, where they occur, and to support their subsequent federation or networking.

We must recognise cultural plurality. The dominant cultural mechanisms are currently geared to the mass production of a very limited range of

CAPITALISM PROPOSES THE POWER OF DISTRIBUTION

views, emanating from interlocking interests that constitute the ruling class.

This monopoly is maintained by the artificially high costs of access to the media of communication, and by legal restrictions imposed in the name of 'public interest'. These entry costs must be dramatically lowered, and these monopolies must be broken up. These current forms of social control must be replaced by an entirely different form of social accountability geared to promoting pluralities of expression.

We must learn different kinds of responsibility from those used to justify the monopolies of the dominant institutions. We must begin by recognising that cultures arise within groups and are expressed collectively. Groups have a right to express themselves and *communicate* in their own voice and in their own forms. Any notion of 'responsibility' that silences some voices and restricts some forms is clearly oppressive.

Capitalism prevents genuine popular communication and the ability to determine locally the ideas and activities public resources should support. The idea of an abstract 'freedom of speech' is promoted to disguise this. From the perspective of cultural democracy, the issue is not 'freedom of speech' but democratic agreement on the nature of public expression, and democratic control over the means of public expression.

We must abolish any 'standards of excellence' which presume to be universal while being arranged and implemented by the most wealthy, mobile and

52

'educated' within society. The idea of an 'official' set of standards, and a set of regulations to administer them, presents those views which reflect, and favour, the interests of one class as a 'balanced' and, by implication, 'natural' common-sense, to which all groups and all classes should aspire.

The strength of the ruling classes is that they are an interlocking set of interests rather than an identifiable group of people, and thus the dominant culture which they have brought into being, and which it nurtures and promotes, functions by fostering and sustaining a set of beliefs and ideas which support and legitimlse those interests. Cultural democracy is a way of breaking up and replacing that imposed culture with cultures which are open, accessible and plural.

These democratic cultures allow people to develop and communicate social meanings within their own lives, and to participate in the creation and administration of democracy, rather than swallow the illusion of democracy which capitalism fosters to preserve itself.

We must build visible, flexible networks that will support the exchange of these ideas, through a growing number of conditional and contingent alliances. We must ensure that these networks are powerful enough to build democracy: cultural democracy, industrial democracy, political democracy.

Many strands of the activities that comprise cultural democracy already exist. The foundations of many alliances have been laid. We believe the key element in creating cultural democracy is making apparent how and why some of its many component strands are operating and why others need to be brought into play.

The leap that creates a social movement from the practice of many groups begins with this commitment to opening up the means by which we determine our goals. We aim to make accessible our potential to ally with others.

Languages are the means of our expression. They are social frameworks as much as schools or factories. We are all producers and all consumers. As cultural activists we need to establish democratic control of the languages we use, from English to road signs.

Education, however it takes place, is the means by which we learn to use expression. We believe education should primarily be about ways of thinking, not about subjects of thought. It should emphasise the skills of sharing experience and of applying what is learned. We need to clarify how education is originated, what is chosen to be taught, how and by whom. It is essential that those decisions are democratic.

We need educational resources, defined by communities, where anyone can share education, rather than institutions for specific groups to receive instruction. These resources should not be restricted by any arbitrary criteria such as age.

OUR FUTURE

Our premise for action emphasises translating personal experience into cultural activity, rather than the uniformity of defining work according to exterior goals. Our intention is to do this democratically, by negotiation not imposition. The equality we aim for has no meaning if it is not located in its social contexts.

We seek to create social equality in partnership with those with whom we work. We aim to address both specific oppressions and their roots within the pervasive domination of an international capitalist culture.

We believe that codes of aesthetics, and their interpretion, represent exterior standards of cultural value, and need to be replaced by democratic pluralism. We seek to define and utilise democratic, collaborative methods of working. Without these, 'collectivity' remains abstract and impractical.

We seek abolition of ownership of control, from professional assumptions of ability to the practice of copyright. Public control of the power to distribute through decentralised means needs to be established. The control of any resource can be decentralised - the challenge to us is to implement this ourselves wherever we possess resources.

The implementation of cultural democracy must involve developing ways of overcoming the pitfalls to our organisation of expression. Such pitfalls separate our social purposes from actions. Without resolving these difficulties our activities will support the hidden agendas of the dominant culture. We will entrench rather than replace standard values.

Our work should not limit itself to expressions of

personal taste. We need to ask whether our working partnerships move towards the creation of vocal, visible and enfranchised minorities, in a movement of alliances.

We need to ensure that the organisation of trades unions does not set up a primacy of workers' needs over other social needs. We should not prevent access to communication. We should socialise not professionalise. Protecting our particular interests should not hinder the general democratic development of public services, and the public determination of what those services should be.

Socialism is not antithetical to management, it is the use of management for democratic ends. Political activism is not confined to political parties: it occurs through the generation of social markets which have still largely unrecognised powers of change.

The women's movement is one powerful demonstration of a social market in which value is made and exchanged. We need to develop the management and organisational skills to exchange between such specific social markets.

We must work together to build a future we can call our own. The only alternative is no future, and that is no alternative.

The Shelton Trust is a democratic membership organisation that has grown from within the English and Welsh community arts movement to embrace a wide range of cultural activists. It is engaged in campaigning on issues of cultural democracy, at both local and national levels.

Members of the Trust are engaged in the formation of cultural alliances within trades unions, education, broadcasting and 'the arts'. They participate in the development of the Trust's policies and campaigning activities through local and regional meetings organised around specific goals and targets. They also have access to the Trust's growing information network.

The trust organises an annual conference, as well as regular regional seminars. It publishes *Another Standard* six times a year.

In the last eighteen months the magazine has included interviews with Sheila Rowbotham, Tony Wilson, Maureen O'Farrell, Nabil Shaban, Geoff Travis and Faroukh Dhondy. It has included articles on topics ranging from the use of imagery during the miners' strike to the role of women in the cultural workplace, from the politics behind the Video Recordings Act to the history and practice of Queenspark Books in Brighton.

Membership of the Shelton Trust currently costs £10 per year. For further details please write to: Membership, The Shelton Trust, The Old Tin School, Collyhurst Road, Manchester M10.

This Manifesto was written for the Shelton Trust's campaign for cultural democracy. It was produced as a special issue of **Another Standard.** It was launched and discussed at a Conference held at Sheffield Polytechnic on July 12th and 13th, 1986.

The ideas in this manifesto evolved during the three and a half years preceding the Conference. They developed as a part of the debate and discussion that arose within the series of regional seminars organised by the Shelton Trust.

We would like to thank **Phil Cope** of Valley and Vale Community Arts who started the ball rolling.

The Conference was organised by working parties comprising members and directors of the Trust. The working parties were as follows:

The Organisers of the Manifesto were:

Owen Kelly: member of Mediumwave and author of Community Art and The State.

John Lock: researcher with the Docklands Forum and a Labour Councillor in the London Borough of Newham.

Karen Merkel: member of Cultural Partnerships and freelance researcher.

The manifesto was written collaboratively. The following people contributed at various stages to the different drafts:

Sheila Henderson, Rod Henderson, Felicity Harvest, Debra Reay, Hania Janiurek, Sue Burd, Frank Boyd, Tim Applebee, Tammy Bedford, Andrew Howard.

APPENDIX 2

The Manifesto was designed and laid out by **Andrew Howard, Hania Janiurek** and **Henry Iles.**

The illustrations in the manifesto are based upon a series of pre-hispanic Mexican Stamp designs. These ceramic stamps were used on textiles, banners and as a form of symbolic folk medicine. They formed a significant part of many social and religious rituals. In many ways they constituted the printing presses and the means of public communication in a civilisation based more around images than words.

The Shelton Trust would like to thank **Frank Boyd** of Cultural Partnerships for organising a crash course in computerised typesetting.

The Organisers of the Conference programme and administration were:

Tim Applebee: lecturer in Drama at Bradford and Ilkley Community College and free lance Theatre Director.

Sybil Burgess: freelance administrator and researcher.

Sylvia King: member of Jubilee Community Arts and singer and performer.

The Shelton Trust is grateful to all those who spoke on the conference panels and chaired workshops and discussions. We would also like to thank all the groups and organisations who participated in the displays and exhibitions.

The Shelton Trust would like to thank all the individuals and organisations who provided the support work throughout the conference. In particular, we would like to thank those who organised the creche and the stewarding.

59

The organisers of the Conference Entertainments were:

Jon Sharrocks: student of Community Studies at Bradford and Ilkley Community College.

Mike McCarthy: actor-member of Sheffield Popular Theatre and freelance theatre director and performer.

The Shelton Trust would like to thank all of the performers and musicians for providing the conference entertainment.

The organisers of the Design and Publicity were:

Tammy Bedford: member of Valley and Vale Community Arts, administrator.

Brendan Jackson: member of Jubilee Community Arts, video maker and designer.

Andrew Howard: worker at Islington Bus Company, printer and designer.

Philip Sky: worker at U-Print, Chapter Arts Centre, printer and designer.

The organisers of the finances were:

Pam Gill: worker at Derby Community Photography, photographer.

Anna Potten: member of Mobile Arts, freelance visual designer in Hampshire.

Gary Wiltshire: worker at The Block Project, Community Educationalist.

The Trust would like to thank the following organisations who have given time and resources freely:

Jubilee Community Arts

Mediumwave

Islington Bus Company

Cultural Partnerships

Bradford and Ilkley Community College

Chapter Video Project

Community Arts Workshop

Valley and Vale Community Arts

The Shelton Trust is grateful to those Regional Arts Associations, Trades Unions and Local Authorities who offered bursaries to assist people to attend the conference. We would like to thank all the organisations and institutions who gave donations and financial support.

The Shelton Trust is slightly supported by the Arts Council of Great Britain.

Book List

Other titles from Comedia

Organizations and Democracy Series